A Day in the Desert

To all of the future authors and illustrators
in classrooms everywhere

ROBERT TAYLOR ELEMENTARY SCHOOL
MISSION STATEMENT

Robert L. Taylor's staff, students, parents and community, recognizing that
ALL students can learn, will assure the academic, physical and emotional
development of ALL students in a safe, supportive environment.

Published by Willowisp Press
801 94th Avenue North, St. Petersburg, Florida 33702

Printed in the United States of America

2 4 6 8 10 9 7 5 3

ISBN 0-87406-686-7

A Day in the Desert

WRITTEN AND ILLUSTRATED BY THE FIRST-GRADE STUDENTS OF
ROBIN FOLLMER, DALE SEGAL-KRAL, AND CHRISTINA SEITZ
AT ROBERT TAYLOR ELEMENTARY SCHOOL, HENDERSON, NEVADA

Jason Albright, Michael Anderson, Rebecca Balzen, Keri Bybee, Anthony Chavez, T. J. Click, Courtney Crabtree, Tara Danaher, Chris Dechene, Manuel Duque, Richard Fresquez, April Fyke, Jimmy Garfield, Santana Gonzales, Rhiannon Guthery, Jackie Hamblin, Chasity Harper, Kevin Harper, Melissa Heil, Ernesto Hepker, Ricky Hernandez, Zachary Hippler, Alexis Hooper, Daniel Hutcherson, Natasha Kennedy, Jeremy Marsden, Darrell McLaughlin, James Mungai, Amanda Palmer, Josie Pomering, Steven Ruelas, Gregory Shoels, Savannah Simms, David Sotelo, Kindra Twitchell.

About
A Day in the Desert . . .

When we heard of the Kids Are Authors™ Competition, our class decided that we should write about something important that we knew a good deal about, and wished to share with other children. We considered many topics before choosing the desert. Since we had just studied the state of Nevada (and celebrated Nevada's admission day of October 31, 1864), our students had a good deal of information they felt they could share about the beauty of the place which we call home, the Mojave Desert.

The illustrations were created using a crayon-resistant watercolor technique—a favorite of our first graders.

It is morning in the desert.
The sun rises over the mountain.
The sky turns blue.

The giant cactus grows fruit and flowers.

The jackrabbit hops to
his home in the desert.

The rattlesnake rattles
his tail in the morning.
He looks for a kangaroo rat for breakfast.
The kangaroo rat hides under the sagebrush.

At noon, the sun is high in the sky and it is hot. The lizard's skin protects it from the hot sun.

A woodpecker pecks
at a Joshua tree.

The roadrunner doesn't
need to drink water.
He gets his
water from
his food.

A desert tortoise walks slowly through the rocks.

The sun goes down.
The desert sky turns purple, then black.
The stars are bright in the night sky.

The desert animals
come out to look for food.
The full moon is white.
The owl hoots at night from
his hole in the giant cactus.

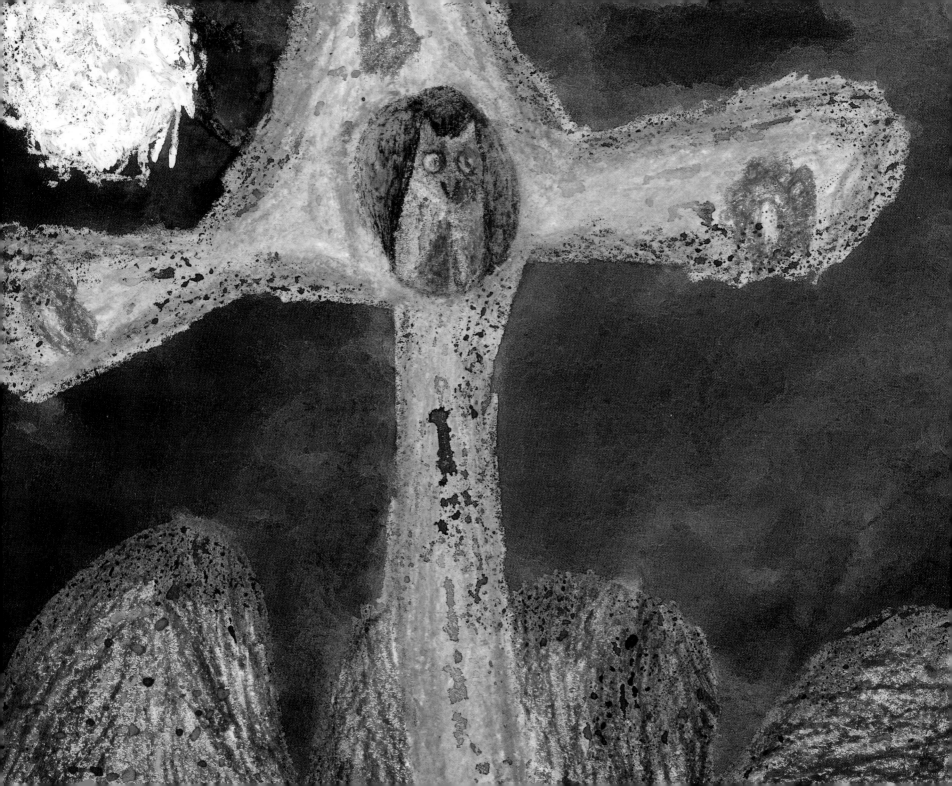

The animals' songs
fill the cool night air.

 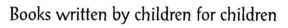 **Kids Are Authors**™

COMPETITION

Books written by children for children

School Book Fairs established the Kids Are Authors™ Competition in 1986 to encourage children to read

and to become involved in the creative process of writing. Since then, thousands of children have written,

designed, and illustrated their own books as participants in the Kids Are Authors™ Competition.

The winning books in the annual competition are published by Willowisp Press®

and distributed in the United States and Canada.

For more information on the
Kids Are Authors™ Competition write to:

IN THE U.S.A.,	IN CANADA,
School Book Fairs, Inc.	Great Owl Book Fairs
Kids Are Authors™ Competition	Kids Are Authors™ Competition
801 94th Avenue North	257 Finchdene Square, Unit 7
St. Petersburg, Florida 33702	Scarborough, Ontario M1X 1B9

PUBLISHED WINNERS IN THE ANNUAL
KIDS ARE AUTHORS™ COMPETITION

1993: **A Day in the Desert** (U.S. winner) by first graders of Robert Taylor Elementary School, Henderson, Nevada.
    The Shoe Monster (Canadian winner) by first and second graders of North Shuswap Elementary School, Celista, British Columbia.

1992: **How the Sun Was Born** (U.S. winner) by third graders of Drexel Elementary School, Tucson, Arizona.
    The Stars' Trip to Earth (Canadian winner) by eighth graders of Ecole Viscount Alexander, Winnipeg, Manitoba.

1991: **My Principal Lives Next Door!** by third graders of Sanibel Elementary School, Sanibel, Florida.
    I Need a Hug! (Honor Book) by first graders of Clara Barton Elementary School, Bordentown, New Jersey.

1990: **There's a Cricket in the Library** by fifth graders of McKee Elementary School, Oakdale, Pennsylvania.

1989: **The Farmer's Huge Carrot** by kindergartners of Henry O. Tanner Kindergarten School, West Columbia, Texas.

1988: **Friendship for Three** by fourth graders of Samuel S. Nixon Elementary School, Carnegie, Pennsylvania.

1987: **A Caterpillar's Wish** by first graders of Alexander R. Shepherd School, Washington, D.C.

1986: **Looking for a Rainbow** by kindergartners of Paul Mort Elementary School, Tampa, Florida.